HOT

Celebrity Biographies

Michael Phelps

SWIMMING FOR OLYMPIC GOLD

BY DAVID P. TORSIELLO

 Enslow Publishers, Inc.
40 Industrial Road
Box 398
Berkeley Heights, NJ 07922
USA
http://www.enslow.com

For my parents,
Ann and Pat Torsiello

Library of Congress Cataloging-in-Publication Data

Torsiello, David P.
   Michael Phelps : swimming for Olympic gold / David P. Torsiello.
      p. cm. — (Hot celebrity biographies)
   Includes index.
   Summary: "A biography of American Olympic swimmer Michael Phelps. In 2008, he won eight gold medals at the
      Olympic Games in Beijing, breaking the record of most gold medals won at a single Olympics"—Provided by
      publisher.
   ISBN-13: 978-0-7660-3591-1
   ISBN-10: 0-7660-3591-3
   1. Phelps, Michael, 1985–   —Juvenile literature. 2. Swimmers—United States—Biography—Juvenile literature.
   I. Title.
   GV838.P54T67 2009
   797.2'1092—dc22
   [B]
                            2008048700

Paperback ISBN-13: 978-0-7660-3630-7
Paperback ISBN-10: 0-7660-3630-8

Printed in the United States of America

10 9 8 7 6 5 4 3 2 1

To Our Readers: We have done our best to make sure all Internet Addresses in this book were active and appropriate when we went to press. However, the author and publisher have no control over and assume no liability for the material available on those Internet sites or on other Web sites they may link to. Any comments or suggestions can be sent by e-mail to comments@enslow.com or to the address on the back cover.

♻ Enslow Publishers, Inc., is committed to printing our books on recycled paper. The paper in every book contains 10% to 30% post-consumer waste (PCW). The cover board on the outside of each book contains 100% PCW. Our goal is to do our part to help young people and the environment too!

Cover Illustration: AP/Wide World Photos.

Photos and Illustrations: AP/Wide World Photos, pp. 1, 17, 20, 27, 30, 33, 41; Bernd Thissen/ dpa/ Landov, p. 34; David Gray/ Reuters/ Landov, p. 26; Getty Images, pp. 13, 23, 24, 40; Joe Rimkus, Jr./ MCT/ Landov, p. 4; Peter Parks/ AFP/ Getty Images, p. 28; Reuters/ Mark J. Terrill/ Landov, p. 22; Sports Illustrated/ Getty Images, pp. 29, 39; Wolfgang Rattay/ Reuters/ Landov, p. 7.

Contents

A Fantastic Finish

A little more than half a second. . . . A blink of an eye for most of us. . . . But in a swimming race it is an eternity. This was the difference between Michael Phelps and Milorad

◄ *Michael Phelps closes in on Milorad Cavic during the 100-meter butterfly in the 2008 Summer Olympic Games in Beijing, China, on August 16, 2008.*

Cavic of Serbia halfway through the 100-meter butterfly at the 2008 Olympics—.62 of a second, to be exact.

Cavic was in the lead. Phelps was in seventh place. Fifty meters to go. But just when many others would have given up, Phelps began to surge. "That's why he's the king," one of the team coaches later said. One after another, Phelps swam past the competition. Soon only Cavic was left ahead of him. A lot was on the line. At stake were millions of dollars, national pride, personal glory, and Olympic immortality.

Back in 1972 American swimmer Mark Spitz set an Olympic record when he won seven gold medals. The photo of Spitz draped in his seven golds became an iconic image. Before Michael Phelps came along, Spitz's record seemed unbreakable. But Phelps was a genuine threat. In 2004 swimwear company and Olympic sponsor Speedo had offered Phelps a one-million-dollar prize for matching Spitz's record. Phelps fell just short that year. Now, four years later, he was determined to make history. Phelps had taken the gold in his first six events. Now Cavic was all that stood in his way.

ONE ONE-HUNDREDTH OF A SECOND

As Phelps and Cavic approached the wall the race was too close to call. At the very end Phelps snuck in an added, desperate half stroke. To the naked eye, it appeared the swimmers touched the wall at the same time. Many assumed Cavic had held on to win—including Bob Bowman. Even Phelps's mother, watching in the stands, held up two fingers as if to say, "second place."

Everyone in the building turned their heads and fixed their eyes on the scoreboard. It seemed to take forever for the times to appear. When they did, Phelps's time was listed as 50.58 seconds. Cavic's was 50.59 seconds. Phelps had won by one one-hundredth of a second. When Phelps realized this, he thrust his fists in the air and shouted with joy.

"I had to take my goggles off first to make sure the one [signifying first place] was next to my name," Phelps later said. "That's when I sort of let out my roar."

The Serbian coach appealed the decision but accepted the ruling after reviewing photos immediately after the race. Several days later, a digital photo sequence was released to the public to confirm the results. Timer Silvio Chianese observed that, "This is the only sport where athletes don't

▲ *Phelps (left) sneaks in an extra half-stroke while Cavic (right) glides to the wall. Phelps ended up winning by one one-hundredth of a second.*

cross the finish line. The athlete stops." Swimmers have to touch a pad on the wall to determine their times. Chianese explained that it takes 6.6 pounds (3 kilograms) of pressure to activate the pad. "Any less and waves [from the water] would set it off."

"When I saw the replay," Phelps said, "when I did that extra half stroke, I thought that I'd lost the race. But I guess when I took the half stroke, that was what I needed."

THE IMPOSSIBLE DREAM

Michael Phelps had overcome a great deal to reach these heights. As a child, he suffered from Attention Deficit Hyperactivity Disorder (ADHD). He also had to struggle to cope with his parents' divorce. At school, the other kids would tease him about his big ears and skinny body. Before learning to swim, he had actually been afraid of the water. And he also watched one of his older sisters struggle with Olympic disappointment.

"I think the biggest thing," Phelps said, "is when someone says you can't do something, when there are big quotes in the paper to say that it's impossible to ever, ever tie or break this record, it just shows you that anything's possible. When you put your mind to something and you really focus on doing it, anything's possible."

With his victory in the 100-meter butterfly, Phelps had tied Spitz's record with one more race yet to swim. Could he really set a new record by earning an eighth gold medal? Well, after his amazing victory in the butterfly, no one would dare say it was impossible.

Michael Phelps was born on June 30, 1985. He is the youngest of three children, born after sisters Hilary and Whitney. His parents, Fred and Debbie, were high school sweethearts. Fred had played football, and Debbie had been a cheerleader. Fred was good enough to set several school records and even tried out for the Washington Redskins of the National Football League (NFL). After they earned their degrees and got married, Debbie became a teacher and Fred a police officer.

As a child, Michael was very energetic. It seemed he could never sit or stand in one place for very long. He always needed to have something in his hands to play with. He was also accident prone. "If it was breakable," Michael recalled, "I usually found it."

GROWING PAINS

Fred and Debbie Phelps separated in 1992. Michael and his sisters had a hard time adjusting to this. Although Fred remained a presence in Michael's life for a time, the two

PERSONAL INFO

Favorite Music: Rap
Favorite Rappers: Lil' Wayne, Young Jeezy, Notorious B.I.G., and Eminem
Favorite Movie: Miracle
Favorite Swimming Stroke: The butterfly
Heroes: His mom & Michael Jordan

slowly drifted apart. As Michael later recalled: "I stopped trying to involve him in my activities and he stopped trying to involve himself."

This same year Michael started taking swimming lessons with the North Baltimore Aquatic Club (NBAC). His first instructor was a woman named Cathy Lears, a family friend and neighbor. At first Michael hated the water. The younger brother of two great swimmers was actually afraid to get his face wet! Swimming was not nearly as much fun as it seemed when he was watching his sisters. Michael would yell and throw tantrums, refusing to cooperate. In order to get him in the pool, Lears started him off with the backstroke. This way his face would not get wet.

After a while Michael started to take to swimming, and his skills developed quickly. Soon he no longer wanted to leave the water. The pool became an escape for Michael. When he was swimming, it took his mind off his parents' divorce. It also helped him escape some of his teasing classmates.

They sometimes made jokes about his large ears. Some of the kids even called him Spock, referring to the *Star Trek* character. Because of this, Michael would often try to hide his ears under his Baltimore Orioles baseball cap.

AN EVENTFUL YEAR

The year 1996 was an eventful one for the Phelps family. This was the year that fifteen-year-old Whitney went to the Olympic trials. But back soreness kept her from swimming her best, and she did not make the team.

At the same time, Michael was struggling. This was the year he started wearing braces. His impulsive nature was also beginning to get the best of him. He was often benched at the pool for misbehaving. At school, one of his teachers said he "wouldn't amount to anything because he couldn't concentrate." This is when Michael was first diagnosed with ADHD.

Perhaps most importantly, 1996 was the year Bob Bowman took over as the swim coach at the Meadowbrook Aquatic & Fitness Center, home of the NBAC. Shortly after Bowman's arrival, Michael set a national record in the 100-meter butterfly for his age group. This was an eye-opener for

ALL IN THE FAMILY

Whitney was the national champ in the women's 200 meter butterfly at age fourteen. Hilary earned a swimming scholarship to the University of Richmond and set several school records there.

Bowman. In the fall of 1997, he approached Michael's parents and told them that their son had the potential to be an Olympic swimmer.

THE DAY IT ALL CHANGED

By March of 2000, at the national championships in Seattle, Michael had cut his time in the 200-meter butterfly by an amazing five seconds, finishing in 1:59. This made him one of the fastest swimmers in the world. And he was just fourteen. "That day changed everything," Bowman recalled.

That same year Whitney and Michael both went to the Olympic trials. Whitney was still swimming at this point, though in great pain due to the bulging disks in her back. (She eventually dropped out of the trials as a result of this.) Meanwhile, Michael was too young to be considered a favorite to make the team. In its trials forecast, *Swimming World* magazine had predicted that he was "probably [still] a year or two away from being a factor on the world scene." So when Michael qualified by finishing second in the 200 butterfly, everyone was shocked. Whitney greeted him after the race with an emotional hug. "It was an amazing thing for a male

▲ *Michael Phelps swims in the heats of the 200 butterfly on Day 3 of the Olympic Games in Sydney, Australia, on September 18, 2000.*

swimmer that age to make the Olympic team," Whitney said. "And he's my little brother; he means the world to me."

THE 2000 GAMES

The 2000 Olympic Summer Games took place in Sydney, Australia, just a little more than a month after Michael's fifteenth birthday. Michael was the youngest member of any U.S. team since 1932. He placed fifth in his one and only event, the 200 butterfly.

Just a short time after Sydney, Michael would have his braces taken off, get his learner's permit . . . and set his first world record.

In the wake of Sydney, Michael set a new goal for himself for extra motivation: At the 2001 Nationals he would break a world record. And he proceeded to do just that. He set a new world record in the 200 butterfly—the same event in which he placed fifth in Sydney. At fifteen years of age, he was the youngest swimmer to ever hold a world record.

2001 WORLDS

Since the Nationals also served as the trials for the World Championships, this meant that Michael would be going to compete in Japan that summer. There, he won the 200 fly again, making him the champion and gold medalist in the event for 2001. He also broke his own record, setting a new world mark of 1:54.58.

MORE SUCCESS

Michael's success continued in 2002. That summer, at the Nationals in Fort Lauderdale, he set an American record in the 200-meter IM (individual medley) and came in just under his own record in the 200 fly. He also won the 400-meter IM. He credited this victory to his touch—"That was the first time I realized that if I nailed the touch at the perfect time, that could make the difference," Michael said.

HOW MANY DOGS?

At the 2003 World Championships in Spain, Michael entered six events: two IMs, two flies, and two relays. In his words, he saw it as "a great dry run for the crowded schedule I might be looking at in Athens." Before leaving home, he got his mom to agree to let him get a dog if he broke a world record at the meet. He met this goal in his very first event, the 200 fly. Up in the stands, Hilary held up a sign that read DOG? Then he set another new world record when he swam in the 200 IM semis. Hilary held up another sign: 2 DOGS? Then he broke his own record in this same event in the finals. 3 DOGS? He would set his fourth and fifth records at Worlds in the 100 fly semis and 400 IM finals. Hilary's last sign: 5 DOGS? Michael finished the meet with five medals (three gold, two silver) and had broken five world records.

PHELPS VS. THORPE

The 200 IM at the 2003 World Championships featured a dramatic matchup. Ian Thorpe had entered the race and it was the first time he and Phelps raced head-to-head. Phelps beat him by over three seconds. Thorpe was two bodylengths behind when Phelps touched the wall.

Just a few weeks after Worlds, Michael swam at the Summer Nationals in College Park, Maryland. Fearing a letdown after his big performance in Spain, Coach Bowman offered a special challenge to keep Michael motivated: If he could finish the 200 IM in under 1:56, Bowman would get his head shaved. Michael ended up touching the wall at 1:55.96. Bowman's hair was gone, along with another world record. It was the seventh world record Michael had broken in a span of just forty-one days.

IN SPITZ'S SHADOW

Just before the 2004 Olympic Trials, Michael's agent came up with an interesting proposal for Speedo: A one-million-dollar bonus for Michael if he could match Spitz's record of seven golds at either the 2004 or 2008 Olympics. Speedo agreed to the proposal. And both sides decided to make the deal public. Michael believed this would be "good for swimming. People would talk about the [million dollars]. They would mention Speedo. The buzz would give the press an extra incentive to write about swimming in advance of the Olympics."

Michael Phelps's first race at the trials was the 400 IM. He won, setting a new record in the process. Next up was the 200-meter freestyle. He won the event with a time of 1:46.27

▲ *Olympic legend Mark Spitz raises the hand of Michael Phelps after Phelps's victory in the 200 fly at the Olympic Trials in Long Beach, California, on July 10, 2004.*

but he was disappointed—he was hoping to finish in the 1:45s. He followed this up with a win in the 200 fly.

The awards ceremony that followed the 200 fly featured a very special presenter: Mark Spitz. This was the first time Spitz and Phelps would meet. Spitz presented Phelps with the winner's medal, raised his hand, and pointed to him while the crowd roared. Phelps later recalled:

> There aren't many things that can make me shake, I mean literally shake, but I could feel goose bumps all the way up and down my arms and legs. . . . That was amazing. I walked away and needed some time to just process the whole thing. He's the greatest icon in the sport, and it was like he was passing the torch to me.

Spitz told reporters afterward: "I think he really has a chance to do this [match his record of seven golds]. That's one of the things I told him. It's a great opportunity for Michael, it's a great opportunity for swimming, and it's also a great opportunity for the Olympics."

Phelps went on to take second in the 200 backstroke, first in the 200 IM, and second in the 100 fly. By placing either first or second in each event, Phelps earned the right to compete at the Olympics in any or all of them. In fact, he was the first athlete in U.S. history to qualify for six individual events.

DREAMS OF GOLD

Phelps would not lack support in Athens. His mother, both sisters, and his father were all there. His first event would be the 400 IM. As Phelps stood on the block waiting for the starter's gun, he wasn't thinking about seven gold medals. He was thinking about just one. "One gold medal," Phelps wrote in his autobiography, *Beneath the Surface*. "That's what I [had] thought about since 1992, the year I realized I could swim."

At the start of the 400 IM, Phelps jumped out to a quick lead—just as he and Bowman had planned. The idea was to have a healthy lead before the breaststroke (Phelps's weakest stroke). As he took his last turn and began the final 50 meters he could see the competition to his left and right were trailing him. It was at that point that Phelps knew he was going to win the gold. He set a new world record with his time. Friend and teammate Erik Vendt finished second to take the silver.

The next day Ian Crocker raced a weak leg for the U. S. in the 4 x 100 freestyle relay. This caused the team to finish third, behind South Africa and The Netherlands, and Phelps had to settle for bronze. There were now six events left, and Phelps would have to take gold in all of them if he wanted to tie Spitz. And his biggest challenge of the games was up next.

"THE RACE OF THE CENTURY"

The day after was the 200 free and the showdown with Australian Ian Thorpe. The press had dubbed it "The Race of the Century" due to all of the great swimmers who would be competing. Phelps finished the race with a time of 1:45.32, which set a new American record . . . but this was only good enough for third place. Thorpe finished first and Pieter van den Hoogenband of The Netherlands took second.

With the third place finish Spitz's record was now out of reach. Most of the questions Phelps faced from the press

◀ *Gold medalist Ian Thorpe (center), silver medalist Pieter van den Hoogenband (left), and bronze medalist Michael Phelps (right) pose with their medals after the 200-freestyle race at the Athens games on August 16, 2004.*

afterward were about no longer being able to reach Spitz. No one seemed to care about the three medals (two bronze, one gold) that he had won. This motivated Phelps to finish strong and silence his critics.

"He's motivated by failure, he's motivated by success," Bob Bowman later said. "He can take just about anything and turn it into some kind of motivation. That's one of his greatest attributes."

ON A ROLL

Next up was the 4 x 200 meter freestyle relay—an event Australia had dominated. They were on a seven-year winning streak, with three straight world titles and four new world records set during that time. But the United States came out strong, led by Phelps. By the start of the anchor leg, they led the Australians by a body length. But Ian Thorpe was swimming the anchor for Australia. He pulled even with American Klete Keller within his first 50 meters. Phelps, who had swum the first leg, was going crazy on the deck with his teammates. "He's out too fast," Phelps said of Thorpe. "He can't hold it."

Sure enough, Thorpe faded briefly and Keller pulled back in front. At the last moment Thorpe made a desperate surge for the wall, but it was not enough. Australia's streak was over—the U.S. had won.

This started Phelps on a roll. He would earn gold in his next three races and set three new individual Olympic records. In just one week Phelps had earned five golds and two bronze. Because one of those golds was in the 100-meter fly, Phelps had earned the right to swim that stroke in the 4 x 100 medley relay. But he decided to offer this spot on the relay team to Ian Crocker instead.

Earlier, in the 4 x 100 freestyle relay, Crocker's weak performance in his leg of the race had cost the team (and Phelps) a possible gold medal. But as Phelps would later say,

"Ian's one of the greatest relay swimmers in history. I was willing to give him another chance." The race would also be Crocker's last chance to earn a gold medal for himself in Athens.

Because Phelps had swum the fly leg in the preliminaries for the event, he would still get a medal if the team won . . . but he was putting his fate in Crocker's hands by giving up his spot. Team coach Eddie Reese called it "a [heck] of a gesture." Crocker considered it "a gift too large to accept." But after some encouragement Crocker agreed to take the spot.

Crocker rewarded Phelps's faith by completing his leg in 50.28 seconds. This was the second-fastest time ever in the

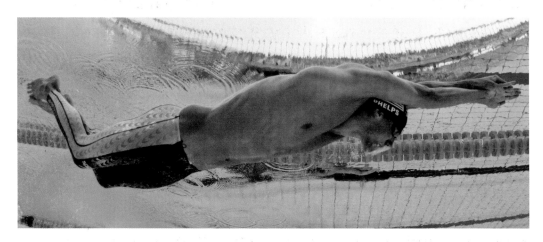

▲ *Phelps swims the 100-meter butterfly at the Athens games on August 20, 2004.*

fly split. Overall, the team set a new world record with its total time of 3:30.68. Crocker had earned his one and only gold medal in Athens. Phelps congratulated Crocker after the race, and Crocker thanked him for having stepped aside. "He gave me a great opportunity," Crocker said.

And Crocker's efforts had given Phelps his sixth gold and eighth medal overall. He may not have matched Spitz's seven golds, but he was still the first person to win eight total medals in a single, non-boycotted Olympics. When it was all over, Phelps was physically and emotionally drained.

"I miss going to breakfast at Pete's [Grill]," he told reporters. "I miss my car. I miss the house. I miss my cat. I miss everything at home."

Phelps was indeed on his way back to Baltimore. But not for very long.

Michigan and More

After the Athens games Phelps and Bowman had planned a move to the University of Michigan. There, Bowman would take over as the school's swimming coach, while Phelps pursued a degree in sports management. Since he was a professional swimmer, Phelps would not be allowed to swim for Michigan's school team, but he would be allowed to train with them.

Shortly before the move, however, Phelps found himself in some trouble. On November 4, 2004, he was pulled over for running a stop sign near Salisbury University in Maryland, where he had gone to visit a friend. Phelps initially denied drinking. But after a few field tests, the officer told him he believed he had been drinking. Phelps then confessed, saying, "I know, I'm sorry. I was just scared because I have a lot to lose."

Phelps pled guilty to drunk driving in court on December 29, 2004. An agreement with prosecutors gave him a sentence of eighteen months probation. Phelps's record would be cleared as long as he complied with his probation. This included making speeches to students at three schools, where he would advise youngsters about making smart decisions and the dangers of drinking and driving.

COLLEGE LIFE

Phelps began taking classes at Michigan in January 2005 while also working as a volunteer assistant for the school's swim team. He enjoyed his time there, both in and out of the water. One of his favorite activities was attending school football games. "I didn't know what to expect coming here," he said. "New place, new friends. But I really like it."

One thing that hadn't changed was his dedication to swimming. Phelps kept working in the pool, and kept the 2008 games in Beijing in his sights at all times.

▼ *Phelps receives instructions from his coach, Bob Bowman.*

GETTING READY FOR BEIJING

Phelps competed in the 2005 World Championships, winning six medals (five gold, one silver) and breaking one Championship record. At the following World Championships two years later (in Australia in April 2007), Phelps won seven gold medals and set five new world records. And

▲ Phelps models the new Speedo LZR Racer swimsuit during a press conference on February 12, 2008. From its release up until the Beijing Games in August, 48 world records were set by swimmers in the suit.

he didn't just break the old records—he wrecked them. In the 400 butterfly he broke his own world record by two full seconds. U.S. head coach Mark Schubert said that Phelps's performance "was the greatest performance of all time. I just didn't notice any weak points. He can do it from behind, he can do it from in front, he can do it when it's close, he can do it when it's not close."

The 400 IM is Phelps's signature event. He has never lost in the event in international competition. He set a world record in the event in 2002 and proceeded to set a new record in it six times after that. During the 2008 Olympic trials in Omaha,

THE DIET

Much has been made of Phelps's amazing appetite. Phelps's typical daily menu (courtesy of the *New York Post*) consists of the following:

Breakfast: Three fried-egg sandwiches loaded with cheese, lettuce, tomatoes, fried onions and mayonnaise. Two cups of coffee. One five-egg omelet. One bowl of grits. Three slices of French toast topped with powdered sugar. Three chocolate-chip pancakes.

Lunch: One pound of enriched pasta. Two large ham and cheese sandwiches with mayo on white bread. Energy drinks packing 1,000 calories.

Dinner: One pound of pasta. An entire pizza. More energy drinks.

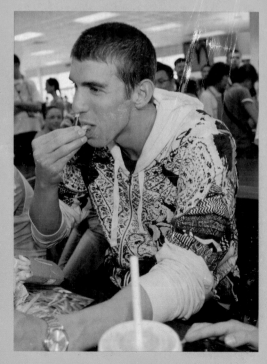

All this adds up to about 12,000 calories a day. Mark Klion, a sports medicine doctor, observed that if Phelps were to eat less, his "body won't recover, the muscles will not recover, there will not be adequate energy stored for him to compete in his next event." Phelps swims at least fifty miles each week in practice. This burns an awful lot of calories. By comparison, cyclists competing in the Tour de France consume about 8,000 to 10,000 calories a day.

▲ *Phelps launches himself into the water during the 400 IM finals at the World Championships in Australia on April 1, 2007.*

Phelps's time was 4:05.25, nearly six seconds faster than his 2002 record.

The key to Phelps's success is his endurance. "I recently calculated how much Michael is going to swim in Beijing," Coach Bowman said. "The total time he'll spend in the water—preliminaries, semifinals, finals, warm-ups, cool-downs—will be the equivalent of running eight or nine marathons over the course of the Olympic Games."

When asked about Phelps's potential, Bowman responded: "Do you reach a point where you can't go any faster? Probably. But I don't think Michael is there yet."

Beijing

On July 23, 2008, just before the games in Beijing, Ian Thorpe (who had retired from swimming in 2006) told Fox News: "I don't think he [Phelps] will win eight gold medals. I don't think he will. But mind you, if there is any person on

◀ Phelps swims in a heat for the 400 IM in Beijing. His exploits in the pool earned Phelps the nickname "American Superfish" by the Chinese media.

the planet who is capable, it is him. It's sad, but I just don't think it will happen."

Not surprisingly, Phelps taped Thorpe's comments to his locker and used them for motivation. "I love that sort of stuff," Phelps said, "and those who doubt me fire me right up, so it's all cool and it actually motivates me."

A TEAM PLAYER

Phelps won his first race in Beijing, the 400 IM, setting a new world record in the process. Coach Bowman called it his best race ever. Phelps's teammate Aaron Peirsol agreed, adding: "That was one of the most amazing swims I've seen in my life. He just blew people away. He's going to be on fire."

Phelps's second race was swum as part of the relay team, the 4 x 100 freestyle. It was the first moment of real drama for Phelps in Beijing. Phelps swam the opening leg, coming up second, .27 of a second behind the world-record pace being set by Australia. By the time of the anchor leg, U.S. teammate Jason Lezak trailed Alain Bernard of France by half a body length very late in the race. But Lezak rallied to swim the fastest split ever—46.06 seconds—to finish first. Susan Casey of *Sports Illustrated* described Lezak's effort as "surreal . . . the aquatic equivalent of a distraught mother lifting a car to save her baby." Lezak's teammates on the deck went crazy—especially Phelps. Phelps's emotional reaction when the U.S. team won would prove one of the most memorable images of the Beijing games.

Phelps told reporters afterward that "the relays are the [most fun] events" for him. "Going up there with four guys, we were really one. We all had to swim the perfect race [to win], and we swam that perfect race today." Questioned about his reaction after the win, he added: "I let out a pretty fierce yell. It just shows how emotional that race was and how excited we were. It was just an amazing race. . . . We had to do everything as a team to win that race, and we did."

SWIMMING INTO HISTORY

Phelps came back to take gold again the very next day in the 200 free—again setting a new world record. A day later in the 200 fly, Phelps's goggles filled with water, effectively blinding him. Phelps had to count his strokes in order to know when to make his turns at the wall. "I was just hoping

▲ *Phelps and his U. S. teammates go wild after their amazing victory in the 4 x 100 freestyle relay at the Beijing Games on August 11, 2008.*

that I was winning," Phelps later remarked. Even under these conditions, he managed to set yet another world record with his time of 1:52.03. Still, Phelps was disappointed. "I know I can go faster than that," he said.

Within an hour he was back in the pool as part of the 4 x 200 meter freestyle relay. The team set a new world record in winning, five seconds ahead of second place and less than seven minutes overall—the first time a team ever finished in under seven minutes. It was Phelps's fifth gold in Beijing and eleventh of his career. This surpassed the career totals of several Olympic legends, including U.S. track star Carl Lewis. "To be at the top with so many great athletes who have walked in these Olympic Games, it's a pretty amazing feeling," Phelps said.

◄ Whitney (left) and Hilary (right) stand alongside their mother, Debbie, in the stands at the National Aquatics Center in Beijing to cheer on Michael during the 2008 Games.

On Day 7 of the games, Phelps set a world record in the 200 IM final and once again had to get right back in the water—this time, less than a half hour later. Although he had raced the same schedule in Athens, he was given more time between events there. This made Phelps's accomplishments in Beijing all the more impressive.

RECORD-KEEPING

Although he won his dramatic race against Cavic, it was the first race in Beijing in which Phelps did not set (or take part in) a new world record. His time of 50.58 seconds was still enough for a new Olympic record, however.

This next race was the now-legendary 100 fly in which he beat Milo Cavic and won his seventh gold to tie Spitz. The bronze medalist in the event, Andrew Lauterstein from Australia, remarked, "That was just a great race to be part of, it was an absolute spectacle." Afterward Phelps told reporters, "I came in here wanting to win as many races as I could and getting as many personal best[s] as I could. I have seven out of seven so far."

STANDING ALONE

Phelps-mania was running wild. By this point Phelps had added 1.5 million fans on the popular social networking site Facebook, surpassing the total of then-presidential candidate

Barack Obama. Phelps looked up the pages of some of his old classmates on the Web site and was amused to see how many mentioned going to school with him. He told NBC's Bob Costas that many of them were the same kids who "picked on me, or made fun of me, or never talked to me. So it's kind of funny, but . . . all the making fun of [me] and everything, I think it made me work harder to get [to] where I am now."

On August 17, Phelps swam in his final event: the 4 x 100 medley relay. When the U.S. men's team won (establishing yet another new world record in the process), it gave Phelps his eighth gold medal. He now stood alone as the all-time record holder for gold medals won in one Olympic Games. "Records are always made to be broken no matter what they are," Phelps said after the race. "Anybody can do anything that they set their mind to."

Mark Spitz agreed. "It's okay, records are made to be broken, including mine," he said. "Thirty-six years is a long time."

THE GREATEST OLYMPIAN EVER?

Australian breastroker Leisel Jones took home two golds and a silver in Beijing. But when asked, she called Phelps's performance "my highlight. I couldn't care less about my own swims." Nine-time medalist from Russia Alexander Popov declared, "He is the best. Admit it. Just write it down: He is the greatest in history."

NBA star Kobe Bryant was in Beijing as a member of the U.S. basketball team. During an off day he decided to go watch Phelps race. Phelps won his fourth and fifth gold medals that day. It was the first time Bryant had attended a swimming event, and he was amazed. Bryant recalled saying to some of the other nearby swimmers, "This can't be normal." They responded: "It's not normal. This is history in the making." Bryant's basketball teammate Carmelo Anthony agreed. He compared Phelps's first six gold medals of the games to Michael Jordan's six NBA championships.

After his performance in Beijing, Phelps towered over every other swimmer (and perhaps every other athlete) in history. In his brilliant career he has broken over thirty world records— so far—in various styles. Going back to the previous Olympic Games in Athens, Phelps has won thirteen straight gold medals. He'll look to extend this streak when the games go to London in 2012. U.S. National Swim Team coach Mark Schubert observed: "I don't know that we'll ever see it [again] in our lifetime. We have to cherish it as we watch it."

After his amazing performance in Beijing, Phelps was featured on the cover of *Sports Illustrated* wearing all eight of his gold medals. The photo was meant to evoke the image of Mark Spitz on the cover of the same magazine in 1972. Phelps said, "When I first was taking it [the photo], I had never had them all on at once, and I never realized how heavy it was. But it was a fun picture."

Phelps was hoping to slow down a bit in the wake of the games, but he still had plenty of commitments that kept him busy. First, he went to New York to accept a grant from VISA on behalf of the YMCA. The grant would help the YMCA of Greater New York expand its swimming programs for kids.

Phelps's charitable efforts did not stop there. He also announced that he would be using the one-million-dollar bonus he had earned in Beijing from Speedo to establish the Michael Phelps Foundation. The foundation's first initiative was an eight-city tour across the United States. The tour would also serve to launch the education program Dream,

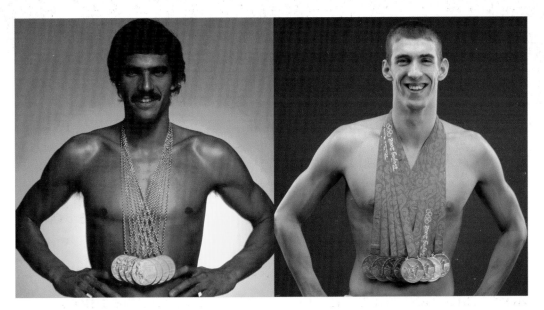

▲ *Mark Spitz with his seven golds in 1972 (left) and Michael Phelps with his eight golds in 2008.*

Plan, Reach. This program is designed not only to promote swimming among young people but to also promote "informed planning and goal-setting, and the importance of personal responsibility and discipline in adhering to that plan in day-to-day living." Speedo also announced an additional $200,000 donation to the foundation "in honor of Michael's eighth gold medal in Beijing."

LIVE FROM NEW YORK . . .

As if this wasn't enough to keep him busy, Phelps also had something else to take care of in New York—hosting the season

◀ *Joe Gromek of Speedo presents Michael Phelps with his $1 million dollar bonus check on September 2, 2008, in New York City.*

premiere of *Saturday Night Live*. Phelps's appearance on the program helped deliver the show a 7.4 rating/18 share, which was a 64 percent improvement over the previous season premiere. In fact, these were SNL's best ratings for a season premiere since 2001 and their best numbers overall since 2002. After being greeted by wild applause at the opening of the show, Phelps thanked the audience and joked, "This seriously is like the ninth greatest moment of my life."

On top of everything else, Phelps also visited London; received a parade at Disney World in Florida; and appeared as a guest at the MTV Video Music Awards. "I usually know where I am," Phelps said of his whirlwind schedule. "I just don't know the date or what day of the week it is. Those are the two things I have trouble with keeping track of."

COMING HOME

Michael Phelps finally returned home to Baltimore by the end of September. There, Phelps accepted a $250,000 grant from Kellogg's cereal company for the Michael Phelps Foundation. At the news conference to announce the grant, Kellogg's unveiled several cereal boxes featuring a photo of Phelps on the front. The conference was held at the Meadowbrook Aquatic & Fitness Center, which Phelps purchased in November.

▲ *Phelps performs his opening monologue on Saturday Night Live while his mother watches from the audience alongside SNL performer Amy Poehler on September 13, 2008.*

"I wanted to come back to Baltimore," Phelps said. "I missed it. This is the place where I grew up and I started everything." Both Phelps and Bowman had decided to leave Michigan to return to Baltimore. Phelps capped off 2008 by being named "Sportsman of the Year" by *Sports Illustrated* in December.

NEW CONTROVERSY

On February 1, 2009, the British tabloid *News of the World* published a photo of Michael Phelps smoking from a water pipe, a device commonly used to inhale marijuana. That same day Phelps admitted that the image was real and apologized. "I engaged in behaviour which was regrettable and demonstrated bad judgment," he said. "For this, I am sorry. I promise my fans and the public it will not happen again."

As a result of the incident, USA Swimming suspended Phelps for three months and Kellogg's announced it would not renew its sponsorship contract with him. Other sponsors, including Speedo, VISA and Hilton Hotels, issued statements of support. "Michael's been through a lot and he's learned a lot, hopefully," Bob Bowman said. "I support him and I want to see him do better."

MOVING FORWARD

Phelps's next immediate goal was to qualify for the World Championships, set to take place in Rome in July 2009. "My mom's told me that I better make the team," Phelps said, "because she wants to go to Rome."

Beyond that, Phelps plans on competing through the Summer Games in London in 2012, when he will be twenty-seven. If he were to win three or more medals there, he would break the record of 18 total medals for one Olympian. Phelps will almost certainly not compete in as many races there as he did in Athens and Beijing, however. He will also train for shorter-distance races, as he does not plan to compete in anything longer than 200 meters. "I think he's more naturally suited to longer events," said Bowman, "so it'll be a change for him, but I think a good one."

And what will come after the London Games in 2012?

"I want to continue with my goal of raising the sport of swimming as high as it can get in the U.S.," Phelps declared. "It won't happen overnight; it will happen over time. I'm ready to be in this for the long haul."

Timeline

1985 June 30: Born in Baltimore.

1992 Parents separate; begins taking swimming lessons.

1999 Swims the junior meet in Orlando, Florida; makes his first national cut.
September: Begins freshman year at Towson High School.

2000 Earns spot on U. S. Olympic team, becoming the youngest U. S. Olympian since 1932.

2001 Sets his first world record (in the 200-meter butterfly).

2004 Wins eight medals (six gold, two bronze) at Olympic Games in Athens.

2008 Wins eight gold medals at Olympic Games in Beijing, breaking Mark Spitz's record of seven golds won at a single Olympics.

Further Info

Books

Phelps, Michael, with Alan Abrahamson. *No Limits: The Will to Succeed*. New York: Free Press, 2008.

Phelps, Michael, with Brian Cazeneuve. *Michael Phelps: Beneath the Surface*. Champaign, Il.: Sports Publishing, LLC, 2008.

DVDs

2008 Olympics: Michael Phelps—Inside Story of the Beijing Games. Ten Mayflower, 2008.

Internet Addresses

SwimRoom: Michael Phelps
http://www.swimroom.com/phelps/

USA Swimming
http://www.usaswimming.org

USA Swimming—Athletes—Michael Phelps
http://swimming.teamusa.org/athlete/athlete/900

North Baltimore Aquatic Club
http://www.nbac.net/

Glossary

anchor—The final swimmer in a relay race.

backstroke—Any style of swimming done face up, on the back. One of the four competitive swimming strokes.

block—The platform a swimmer stands upon prior to the start of a race.

breaststroke—A swimming stroke that is swum by leaning on the chest, with the arms slightly breaking the surface of the water while the legs remain beneath the surface, with the head underwater for the second half of the stroke. One of the four competitive swimming strokes.

butterfly—A swimming stroke where the swimmer is face/chest down and using both arms at once. One of the four competitive swimming strokes.

freestyle—Any unregulated swimming style (but usually the front crawl). One of the four competitive swimming strokes.

front crawl—The standard swimming stroke, where the arms

break the water in alternating fashion (windmill style) while kicking the legs.

lap—A portion of a race consisting of one turn of the course.

leg—Any part of a relay race swum by a single team member.

medley—A swimming event using all four of the competitive swimming strokes on consecutive lengths and equal distances of the race. The order must be butterfly, backstroke, breaststroke, freestyle.

relays—Swimming races in which four swimmers each take a turn completing an equal leg of the race. The two types of relay races in competitive swimming are medley and freestyle.

split—A portion of a race that is shorter than the total distance of the race and is timed. For example, the time a swimmer takes to cover the first 50 meters of a 100-meter race. Multiple splits are often measured for longer distances.

stroke—A style of swimming. There are four strokes in competitive swimming: butterfly, backstroke, breaststroke, and freestyle.

Index